2020

Day Planner

Published by Morningstar Press

unspokengods.com
kmcrawfordarts@gmail.com

October 2019

This book belongs to

Name ________________________________

Phone ________________________________

In case of emergency, please contact

Name ________________________________

Phone ________________________________

National Holidays and Celebrations 2020

January

Wednesday 1 - New Year's Day
Monday 20 - Martin Luther King Jr. Day
Saturday 25 - Chinese New Year

February

Sunday 2 - Groundhog Day
Friday 14 - Valentine's Day
Monday 17 - Presidents' Day
Tuesday 25 - Mardi Gras
- Shrove Tuesday
Wednesday 26 - Ash Wednesday

March

Tuesday 10 - Purim
Tuesday 17 St. Patrick's Day

April

Wednesday 1 - April Fools' Day
Sunday 5 - Palm Sunday
Thursday 9 - Passover
Friday 10 - Good Friday
Sunday 12 - Easter
Monday 13 - Easter Monday
Wednesday 22 - Earth Day
Friday 24 - Ramadan begins

May

Tuesday 5 - Cinco de Mayo
Sunday 10 - Mother's Day
Monday 18 - Victoria Day
Sunday 24 - Eid al-Fitr
Monday 25 - Memorial Day
Friday 29 - Shavuot

June

Sunday 14 - Flag Day
Friday 19 - Juneteenth
Sunday 21 - Father's Day

July

Wednesday 1 - Canada Day
Saturday 4 - Independence Day
Friday 31 - Eid al-Adha

August

Monday 3 - Civic Holiday
Thursday 20 - Muharram begins

September

Monday 7 - Labour Day
Saturday 19 - Rosh Hashanah
Monday 28 - Yom Kippur

October

Saturday 3 - Sukkot
Monday 12 - Thanksgiving Day
- Columbus Day
Thursday 29 - Mawlid al-Nabi
Saturday 31 - Halloween

November

Sunday 1 - All Saints' Day
Monday 2 - All Souls' Day
- Day of the Dead
Wednesday 11 - Remembrance Day
- Veterans' Day
Thursday 26 - Thanksgiving Day

December

Friday 11 - Hanukkah
Friday 25 - Christmas Day
Saturday 26 - Boxing Day
- Kwanzaa
Thursday 31 - New Year's Eve

January - 2020 Month Planner

Sunday	Monday	Tuesday	Wednesday	Thursday	Friday	Saturday
29	30	31	1 New Year's Day	2	3	4
5	6	7	8	9	10	11
12	13	14	15	16	17	18
19	20 Martin Luther King Jr Day	21	22	23	24	25 Chinese New Year
26	27	28	29	30	31	1

February - 2020 Month Planner

Sunday	Monday	Tuesday	Wednesday	Thursday	Friday	Saturday
26	27	28	29	30	31	1
2 Groundhog Day	3	4	5	6	7	8
9	10	11	12	13	14 Valentine's Day	15
16	17 Presidents' Day	18	19	20	21	22
23	24	25 Mardi Gras Shrove Tuesday	26 Ash Wednesday	27	28	29

March - 2020 Month Planner

Sunday	Monday	Tuesday	Wednesday	Thursday	Friday	Saturday
1	2	3	4	5	6	7
8	9	10 Purim	11	12	13	14
15	16	17 St. Patrick's Day	18	19	20	21
22	23	24	25	26	27	28
29	30	31	1	2	3	4

April - 2020 Month Planner

Sunday	Monday	Tuesday	Wednesday	Thursday	Friday	Saturday
29	30	31	1 April Fools' Day	2	3	4
5 Palm Sunday	6	7	8	9 Passover	10 Good Friday	11
12 Easter	13 Easter Monday	14	15	16	17	18
19	20	21	22 Earth Day	23	24 Ramadan begins	25
26	27	28	29	30	1	2

May - 2020 Month Planner

Sunday	Monday	Tuesday	Wednesday	Thursday	Friday	Saturday
26	27	28	29	30	1	2
3	4	5 Cinco de Mayo	6	7	8	9
10 Mother's Day	11	12	13	14	15	16
17	18 Victoria Day	19	20	21	22	23
24 Eid al-Fitr / 31	25 Memorial Day	26	27	28	29 Shavuot	30

June - 2020 Month Planner

Sunday	Monday	Tuesday	Wednesday	Thursday	Friday	Saturday
31	1	2	3	4	5	6
7	8	9	10	11	12	13
14 Flag Day	15	16	17	18	19 Juneteenth	20
21 Father's Day	22	23	24	25	26	27
28	29	30	1	2	3	4

July - 2020 Month Planner

Sunday	Monday	Tuesday	Wednesday	Thursday	Friday	Saturday
28	29	30	1 Canada Day	2	3	4 Independance Day
5	6	7	8	9	10	11
12	13	14	15	16	17	18
19	20	21	22	23	24	25
26	27	28	29	30	31 Eid al-Adha	1

August - 2020 Month Planner

Sunday	Monday	Tuesday	Wednesday	Thursday	Friday	Saturday
26	27	28	29	30	31	1
2	3 Civic Holiday	4	5	6	7	8
9	10	11	12	13	14	15
16	17	18	19	20 Muharram begins	21	22
23 30	24 31	25	26	27	28	29

September - 2020 Month Planner

Sunday	Monday	Tuesday	Wednesday	Thursday	Friday	Saturday
30	31	1	2	3	4	5
6	7 Labour Day	8	9	10	11	12
13	14	15	16	17	18	19 Rosh Hashanah
20	21	22	23	24	25	26
27	28 Yom Kippur	29	30	1	2	3

October - 2020 Month Planner

Sunday	Monday	Tuesday	Wednesday	Thursday	Friday	Saturday
27	28	29	30	1	2	3 Sukkot
4	5	6	7	8	9	10
11	12 Thanksgiving Day Columbus Day	13	14	15	16	17
18	19	20	21	22	23	24
25	26	27	28	29 Mawlid al-Nabi	30	31 Halloween

November - 2020 Month Planner

Sunday	Monday	Tuesday	Wednesday	Thursday	Friday	Saturday
1 All Saints' Day	3 All Souls' Day Day of the Dead	3	4	5	6	7
8	9	10	11 Remembrance Day Veterans' Day	12	13	14
15	16	17	18	19	20	21
22	23	24	25	26 Thanksgiving Day	27	28
29	30	1	2	3	4	5

December - 2020 Month Planner

Sunday	Monday	Tuesday	Wednesday	Thursday	Friday	Saturday
29	30	1	2	3	4	5
6	7	8	9	10	11 Hanukkah	12
13	14	15	16	17	18	19
20	21	22	23	24	25 Christmas Day	26 Boxing Day Kwanzaa
27	28	29	30	31 New Year's Eve	1	2

Important Dates

Notes

Notes

The Year

2020

December - January

MON	
30	
TUE	
31	
WED	
1	
New Year's Day	
THU	
2	

2020

FRI

3

SAT

4

SUN

5

Notes

January

MON
6

TUE
7

WED
8

THU
9

2020

FRI
10

SAT
11

SUN
12

Notes

January

MON
13

TUE
14

WED
15

THU
16

2020

FRI

17

SAT

18

SUN

19

Notes

January

MON
20

Martin Luther King Jr. Day

TUE
21

WED
22

THU
23

2020

	FRI 24
	SAT 25 Chinese New Year
	SUN 26

Notes

January - February

MON

27

TUE

28

WED

29

New Year's Day

THU

30

2020

FRI

31

SAT

1

SUN

2

Groundhog Day

Notes

February

MON
3

TUE
4

WED
5
New Year's Day

THU
6

2020

FRI
7

SAT
8

SUN
9

Notes

February

MON
10

TUE
11

WED
12

THU
13

2020

FRI

14

Valentine's Day

SAT

15

SUN

16

Notes

February

MON

17

Presidents' Day

TUE

18

WED

19

THU

20

2020

	FRI 21
	SAT 22
	SUN 23

Notes

February - March

MON
24

TUE
25

Mardi Gras
Shrove Tuesday

WED
26

Ash Wednesday

THU
27

2020

	FRI 28
	SAT 29
	SUN 1

Notes

March

MON
2
◎

TUE
3

WED
4

THU
5

2020

FRI

6

SAT

7

SUN

8

Notes

March

MON

9

TUE

10

Purim

WED

11

THU

12

2020

	FRI 13
	SAT 14
	SUN 15

Notes

March

MON
16

TUE
17

St. Patrick's Day

WED
18

THU
19

2020

	FRI 20
	SAT 21
	SUN 22

Notes

March

MON 23	
TUE 24	
WED 25	
THU 26	

2020

FRI

27

SAT

28

SUN

29

Notes

March - April

MON
30

TUE
31

WED
1

April Fool's Day

THU
2

2020

FRI

3

SAT

4

SUN

5

Palm Sunday

Notes

April

MON
6

TUE
7

WED
8

THU
9

Passover

2020

FRI

10

Good Friday

SAT

11

SUN

12

Easter

Notes

April

MON
13

Easter Monday

TUE
14

WED
15

THU
16

2020

	FRI 17
	SAT 18
	SUN 19

Notes

April

MON
20

TUE
21

WED
22

Earth Day

THU
23

2020

FRI

24

Ramadan begins

SAT

25

SUN

26

Notes

April - May

MON
27

TUE
28

WED
29

THU
30

2020

	FRI 1
	SAT 2
	SUN 3

Notes

May

MON
4

TUE
5

Cinco de Mayo

WED
6

THU
7

2020

	FRI 8
	SAT 9
	SUN 10 Mother's Day

Notes

May

MON 11	
TUE 12	
WED 13	
THU 14	

2020

FRI

15

SAT

16

SUN

17

Notes

May

MON
18
Victoria Day

TUE
19

WED
20

THU
21

2020

FRI

22

SAT

23

SUN

24

Eid al-Fitr

Notes

May

MON 25 Memorial Day	
TUE 26	
WED 27	
THU 28	

2020

FRI
29
Shavuot

SAT
30

SUN
31

Notes

June

MON
1

TUE
2

WED
3

THU
4

2020

FRI
5

SAT
6

SUN
7

Notes

June

MON
8

TUE
9

WED
10

THU
11

2020

FRI

12

SAT

13

SUN

14

Flag Day

Notes

June

MON
15

TUE
16

WED
17

THU
18

2020

	FRI 19 Juneteenth
	SAT 20
	SUN 21 Father's Day

Notes

June

MON
22

TUE
23

WED
24

THU
25

2020

FRI 26

SAT 27

SUN 28

Notes

June - July

MON
29

TUE
30

WED
1

Canada Day

THU
2

2020

FRI

3

SAT

4

Independence Day

SUN

5

Notes

July

MON
6

TUE
7

WED
8

THU
9

2020

FRI

10

SAT

11

SUN

12

Notes

July

MON
13

TUE
14

WED
15

THU
16

2020

	FRI 17
	SAT 18
	SUN 19

Notes

July

MON
20

TUE
21

WED
22

THU
23

2020

	FRI 24
	SAT 25
	SUN 26

Notes

July - August

MON

27

TUE

28

WED

29

THU

30

2020

FRI

31

Eid al-Adha

SAT

1

SUN

2

Notes

August

MON

3

Civic Holiday

TUE

4

WED

5

THU

6

2020

	FRI 7
	SAT 8
	SUN 9

Notes

August

MON
10

TUE
11

WED
12

THU
13

2020

	FRI 14
	SAT 15
	SUN 16

Notes

August

MON
17

TUE
18

WED
19

THU
20

Muharram begins

2020

	FRI 21
	SAT 22
	SUN 23

Notes

August

MON
24

TUE
25

WED
26

THU
27

2020

	FRI 28
	SAT 29
	SUN 30

Notes

August - September

MON
31

TUE
1

WED
2
○

THU
3

2020

	FRI 4
	SAT 5
	SUN 6

Notes

September

MON

7

Labour Day

TUE

8

WED

9

THU

10

2020

FRI
11

SAT
12

SUN
13

Notes

September

MON 14	
TUE 15	
WED 16	
THU 17	

2020

FRI
18

SAT
19
Rosh Hashanah

SUN
20

Notes

September

MON
21

TUE
22

WED
23

THU
24

2020

FRI
25

SAT
26

SUN
27

Notes

September - October

MON
28

Yom Kippur

TUE
29

WED
30

THU
1

2020

FRI

2

SAT

3

Sukkot

SUN

4

Notes

October

MON
5

TUE
6

WED
7

THU
8

2020

FRI

9

SAT

10

SUN

11

Notes

October

MON
12

Thanksgiving Day
Columbus Day

TUE
13

WED
14

THU
15

2020

	FRI 16
	SAT 17
	SUN 18

Notes

October

MON

19

TUE

20

WED

21

THU

22

2020

FRI

23

SAT

24

SUN

25

Notes

October - November

MON

26

TUE

27

WED

28

THU

29

Mawlid al-Nabi

2020

FRI

30

SAT

31

Halloween

SUN

1

All Saints' Day

Notes

November

MON
2

All Souls' Day
Day of the Dead

TUE
3

WED
4

THU
5

2020

FRI
6

SAT
7

SUN
8

Notes

November

MON
9

TUE
10

WED
11

Remembrance Day
Veterans' Day

THU
12

2020

FRI

13

SAT

14

SUN

15

Notes

November

MON
16

TUE
17

WED
18

THU
19

2020

	FRI 20
	SAT 21
	SUN 22

Notes

November

MON
23

TUE
24

WED
25

THU
26

Thanksgiving Day

2020

FRI
27

SAT
28

SUN
29

Notes

November - December

MON
30

TUE
1

WED
2

THU
3

2020

	FRI 4
	SAT 5
	SUN 6

Notes

December

MON 7	
TUE 8	
WED 9	
THU 10	

2020

FRI

11

Hanukkah

SAT

12

SUN

13

Notes

December

MON

14

TUE

15

WED

16

THU

17

2020

FRI

18

SAT

19

SUN

20

Notes

December

MON
21

TUE
22

WED
23

THU
24

2020

FRI
25
Christmas Day

SAT
26
Boxing Day
Kwanzaa

SUN
27

Notes

December - January

MON
28

TUE
29

WED
30

THU
31

New Year's Eve

2020

FRI

1

New Year's Day

SAT

2

SUN

3

Notes

Notes

Notes

Notes

Notes

Notes

Notes

Notes

Notes

Notes

Printed in Poland
by Amazon Fulfillment
Poland Sp. z o.o., Wrocław

54495150R00078